ABSOLUTE BEGINNERS

Cajon

HAL•LEONARD®

Contact us:

Hal Leonard
7777 West Bluemound Road
Milwaukee, WI 53213
Email: info@halleonard.com

In Europe, contact:
Hal Leonard Europe Limited
42 Wigmore Street
Marylebone, London, W1U 2RY
Email: info@halleonardeurope.com

In Australia, contact:
Hal Leonard Australia Pty. Ltd.
4 Lentara Court
Cheltenham, Victoria, 3192 Australia
Email: info@halleonard.com.au

Order No. AM1007347
ISBN: 978-1-78305-268-4
This book © Copyright 2014 Hal Leonard

Written by Noam Lederman
Edited by Adrian Hopkins
Music processed by Paul Ewers Music Design
Cover and book design by Chloë Alexander
Design Photography by Matthew Ward
Printed in the EU

Music recorded, mixed and mastered by Jonas Persson
Cajon by Noam Lederman
Backing tracks by Jonas Persson
Bass guitar by Tom Farncombe
Additional guitar by Adrian Hopkins

Page 5 image courtesy of
Rubem Dantas
Page 46 images courtesy of
Andrew Lepley/Redferns (Alex Acuna)
Toca Percussion (Nina Rodriguez)
Robert Geary (Ross McCallum)
Lorry Salcedo (Caitro Soto)

Visit Hal Leonard Online at
www.halleonard.com
www.noamlederman.com

*Noam plays Mapex drums, Paiste cymbals, Vic Firth sticks
and Tycoon percussion*

Contents

Introduction

Welcome to *Absolute Beginners Cajon*.
This book is designed for anyone that wants to play the cajon. By working through the book you will learn everything you need to know to perform grooves in various styles, from folk to hip hop. To help you learn, cool backing tracks in each style are provided in this pack to play along with. You will also learn how to choose the right cajon for you, how to produce a good sound and even how to combine the cajon with other percussion instruments.

Whether you are a drummer that is interested in expanding your knowledge of Latin percussion or a complete beginner that has never played an instrument before, this book will suit you. The fundamentals of music notation and basic techniques are explained in detail to allow you to get playing straight away.

The most beautiful thing about this instrument is that it is simple to master the basic sounds, and therefore basic grooves can be achieved within minutes. Then, it is up to you to decide how much you want to practise and how inspired you are to keep researching and progressing.

Congratulations for making the first step into the fascinating world of the cajon, let's begin!

The cajon is a box-shaped percussion instrument that originated in Peru. It is usually played by slapping the front part of the box with the hands and fingers. The cajon can also be played with brushes, mallets or soft sticks. The word *cajon* actually means box, or drawer in Spanish.

The traditional cajon (also referred to as the Peruvian cajon) is usually constructed from plywood. A thinner sheet of plywood on the front acts as the striking surface or head. The modern cajon is built in a similar way, however it usually has snare wires or guitar strings or even bells inside which gives the instrument its distinctive character and helps us create a variety of sounds from the box.

The cajon was most likely developed in Peru during the early 19th century. Over the years it continued to develop and has become an integral part of Peruvian and Spanish music. In 2001 the cajon was awarded "National Patrimony" by the Peruvian National Institute of Culture. Nowadays, it is used worldwide in a variety of styles, including Blues, Pop, Rock, Funk, Jazz and even Drum 'n' Bass.

One of the most significant modern musicians that assisted in the development of the cajon is Spanish guitarist Paco de Lucía. Paco was introduced to the cajon in the 1970s by Peruvian composer and cajon master Caitro Soto. He then used the cajon in his music with the famous Brazilian percussionist Rubem Dantas as his main cajon player.

▼ Rubem Dantas

How to choose your cajon

Which Instrument?

The two main cajons on the market are the Peruvian cajon and the Spanish cajon. The Peruvian cajon has no snare system or wires and therefore its sound is simply the sound of a wooden box. Most modern cajons follow the Spanish cajon system of having either snare wires, guitar strings, or bells attached behind the playing surface.

It is important that you think about the styles of music you are intending to use the cajon for when choosing an instrument. If you intend to play the cajon in a Rock, Funk or a Hip Hop style you will require a solid and punchy bass tone as well as a snare tone that cuts through. Therefore, a Spanish cajon with snare wires will be perfect. However, if you are planning on using the cajon for traditional Latin music, the Peruvian cajon might be better. Most modern cajons have snare wires but these can easily be dampened to reduce their effect. In some cajons the tension of the snare wires can be adjusted in order to create a variety of different sounds.

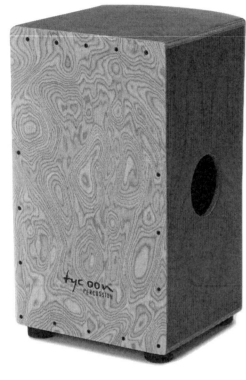

◀ Peruvian cajon

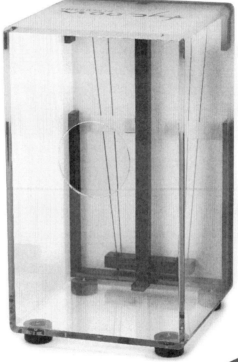

◀ Spanish cajon, showing the snare wires

◀ Spanish cajon

Although cajons are traditionally made from plywood, there are also a variety of instruments available that are made from acrylic.

In today's market you will be able to find many cajon brands with various shapes and tones. It is important that you try playing the cajon before buying it, as much of your decision depends upon personal taste and the style of music you intend to play. Obviously, you need to decide on a budget and then find the most suitable cajon for your needs that you can afford.

Companies such as Tycoon, De Gregorio, Meinl, Latin Percussion and Schlagwerk offer a wide variety of cajons but you should also check out some of the smaller authentic brands such as Duende, Pepote and Lindo Platanus before making your decision.

Buying online might be slightly cheaper, but you will not get a chance to try the instrument before making your decision which could be crucial.

Looking after your cajon is also important. Like any wooden instrument it can react to extreme heat or cold, so aim to store it in moderate temperatures. It is also recommended to invest in a cajon case, so that it is protected while transporting it from place to place.

If you intend to travel much with your cajon you might want to consider a smaller version of the instrument. This is usually referred to as a mini cajon or travel cajon. Many travel cajons come with a suitable stand; they are too small to sit on.

  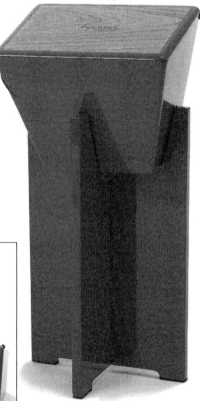

Parts of the cajon

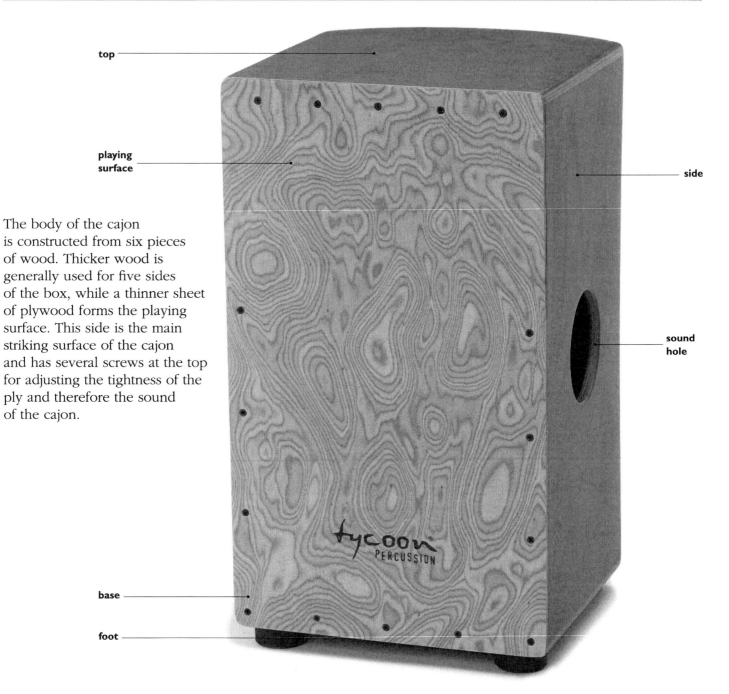

top

playing surface

side

sound hole

The body of the cajon is constructed from six pieces of wood. Thicker wood is generally used for five sides of the box, while a thinner sheet of plywood forms the playing surface. This side is the main striking surface of the cajon and has several screws at the top for adjusting the tightness of the ply and therefore the sound of the cajon.

base

foot

▼ Close up of playing surface corner

▼ Adjusting the tightness of the ply is easy

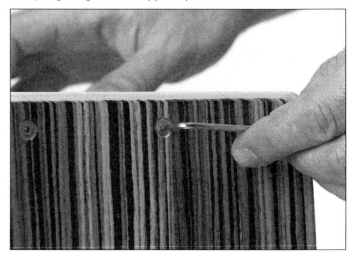

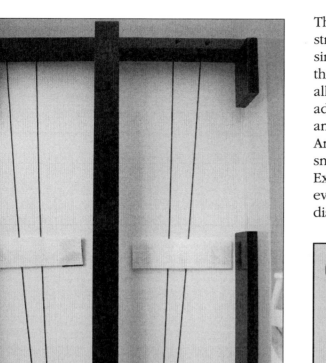

The Spanish cajon has metal wires that touch the striking surface from the back. These wires are very similar to the snare wires on a snare drum. Although the method may vary from instrument to instrument, all cajons with snare wires will have some way of adjusting the sound according to your personal taste and the requirements of the music that you play. Another useful tip is to dampen with tape part of the snare wires to achieve less rattle and a darker tone. Experiment and find your own sound! Some cajons even have bells or little cymbals inside that create a distinctive sound.

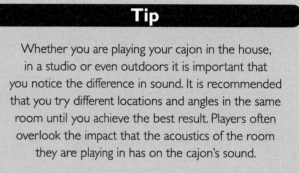

Tip

Whether you are playing your cajon in the house, in a studio or even outdoors it is important that you notice the difference in sound. It is recommended that you try different locations and angles in the same room until you achieve the best result. Players often overlook the impact that the acoustics of the room they are playing in has on the cajon's sound.

◀ Dampened snare wires

▼ Half loose snare wires

▼ Completely loose snare wires

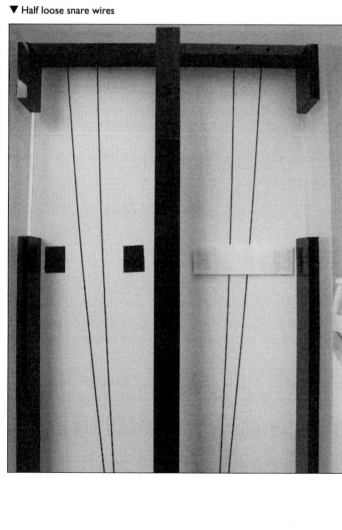

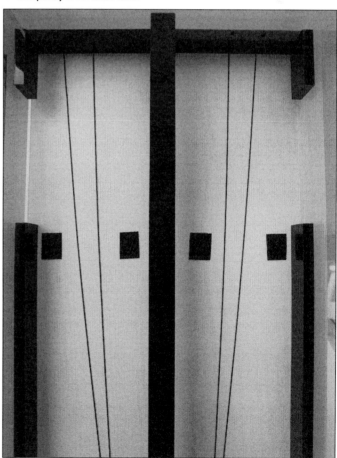

Posture

When starting to play the cajon it is important to find a balanced and comfortable way to sit on the box. It is vital to keep a straight back and ensure that your shoulders are relaxed. Don't be tempted to slouch backwards, lean too far forward, and keep your centre of balance in the middle rather than to one side or the other.

Tip

Your feet should be flat on the floor while playing.

You might find it easier to play if you lift the cajon slightly, so that the striking surface is angled. You may find that this improves the bass tone of the instrument. If playing at a slight angle works for you, there are a few products on the market that are designed to fit under the cajon and hold it in this position.

The hand positions that are used to create specific sounds from the cajon will be discussed from page 14. However, it is recommended that you spend some time to understand the general placement of your hands when playing.

Place your hands naturally on the cajon and ensure that the whole arm, hand, wrist and fingers are relaxed. Like any percussion instrument, practice softly to start with and only start hitting harder when you feel comfortable with your posture and hand positions. This will ensure that you develop secure technique and avoid injury.

Tip

Why not use a mirror to see how your playing looks?

✗ Tensed shoulders

✗ Tensed forearms

✔ Relaxed posture

Rhythms and music notation

Understanding rhythm and drum beats

If you're new to playing, it's going to be useful to spend some time understanding the fundamentals of rhythm, beats and reading rhythmic notation. Although you might choose to learn the cajon just by listening to the examples and learning them from memory, as the grooves become more complex it is helpful to be able to read the rhythms.

To start with, let's look at the idea of *pulse*. The vast majority of musical styles have an underlying pulse or beat – this is what you might tap your foot along to. That beat is divided into regular units, typically of four beats. So you might count along to the music: **1**, **2**, **3**, **4**, **1**, **2**, **3**, **4**. Certain beats – in most styles of music '1' and '3' – are felt as 'strong'. We call these the downbeat. Beats '2' and '4' form the upbeat, or backbeat. Try counting along to a favourite record, emphasising '1' and '3', and this will soon feel natural.

In a band, the beat is provided by the drummer. The three main components of a drum kit are the hi hat cymbals, which keep the basic pulse; the bass drum, which emphasises the downbeat, and the snare drum, which marks the backbeat. Listen to this example of a drum kit rhythm; hopefully this sounds familiar from music you may have heard!

 Track 1: (Drum Beat)

When starting to play cajon, we can emulate the parts of a drum kit to create effective rhythms. So, we have different strokes on the box to mimic the bass drum, snare drum and hi hat.

 Track 2: (Cajon Beat)

Notation

Rhythms are notated using specific symbols to represent each hit, or note, that you play. The basic unit of rhythm is the quarter note, which corresponds to the four beats in the bar. Notes are written on a five line *stave*. They look like this:

Quarter notes

The basic beat can be subdivided to create more rhythmic combinations, into two – or eighth notes:

Eighth notes

Three, or triplets:

Eighth note triplets

And four, or sixteenth notes:

Sixteenth notes

 Listen to tracks 3-6 to hear each type of rhythm count against the basic pulse.

So that the different sounds of the cajon – bass, snare and hi hat – can be notated, symbols are shown on different lines of the musical stave to represent each stroke:

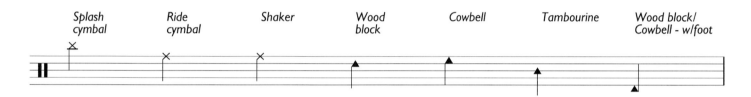

Bass drum
Bass tone

Snare drum
Slap tone

Hi-hat
Soft high pitch tone

Later in the book, we'll look at adding further percussion instruments to your grooves. These have their own positions on the stave:

Splash cymbal   *Ride cymbal*   *Shaker*   *Wood block*   *Cowbell*   *Tambourine*   *Wood block/ Cowbell - w/foot*

General Music Notation

Here are some other signs and symbols that you'll see in the music in this book:

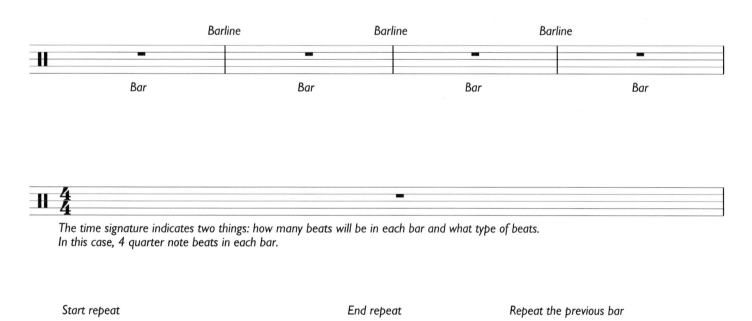

Barline   *Barline*   *Barline*

Bar   *Bar*   *Bar*   *Bar*

The time signature indicates two things: how many beats will be in each bar and what type of beats. In this case, 4 quarter note beats in each bar.

Start repeat   *End repeat*   *Repeat the previous bar*

The first stroke: Bass stroke

The first stroke that you need to learn is the bass stroke. This stroke emulates the bass drum part that is prominent in most drum beats. In order to play a bass stroke, simply flatten your hand and hit the cajon with your palm. Start with your right hand and aim to strike the playing surface about a third of the way down, as shown in the pictures.

Tip
Remember that your hands must be relaxed and not tense. Any stress in the hands will affect the sound you make and might lead to aches and pains.

 Listen to examples 7 & 8 in order to hear the sound you're aiming for.

Although the exact spot on the playing surface will depend on your instrument and personal technique, ensure that you don't try to play the bass too low. Remember we are always looking for the most efficient movement when playing, as this will allow you to play faster and for longer periods of time.

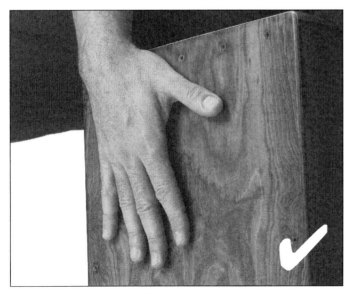

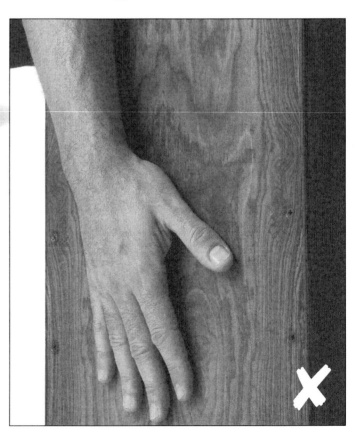

Now, let's focus on achieving the best sound out of this stroke and learn some basic hand combinations. Practise each exercise slowly and continuously until it feels and sounds right. You will notice that there are some rests in these exercises. This means that there is nothing to play on those beats. However, we must always remember that the full value of the rest must be accounted for.

These exercises can be played with the backing tracks that are provided in this book. If you're not using the track, make sure you practise with a metronome. A metronome is a device that helps us maintain a consistent pulse. There are lots of metronomes available on the market for you to choose from.

The letter **R** (**right**) and **L** (**left**) above the exercises indicate which hand should be used when. If you are left-handed you'll need to invert the suggested hand combinations.

Tip

Cupping the striking hand can help you create a fuller bass stroke sound.

Bass stroke exercises 1-4

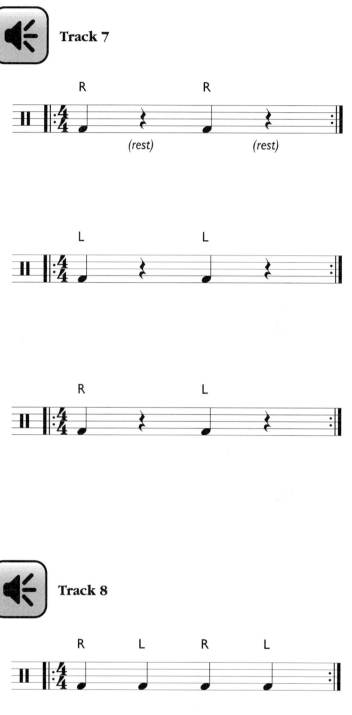

Track 7

Track 8

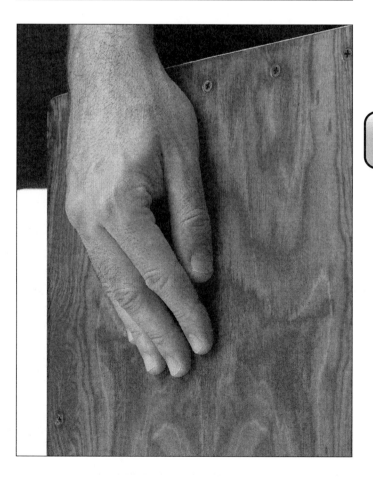

The second stroke: Snare stroke

The snare stroke can also be referred to as a 'slap' or slap stroke. The slap on the cajon is similar to the rim shot sound that can be produced from a snare drum. It will give us the sharp accent that is so important when creating the backbeat of any groove. The backbeats are the second and fourth beats in each bar.

To play the slap you use your arm as well as a slight whipping motion in the wrist. The striking position will vary slightly depending upon your instrument.

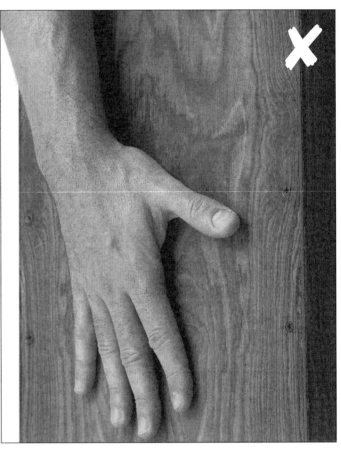

Ensure that you don't play the snare stroke too low, as this can sound like a bass stroke.

After hitting the snare stroke, let your hand bounce back off the cajon. This will help you prepare for the next stroke as well as ensuring that you produce the best sounding stroke without dampening the natural sound of the cajon.

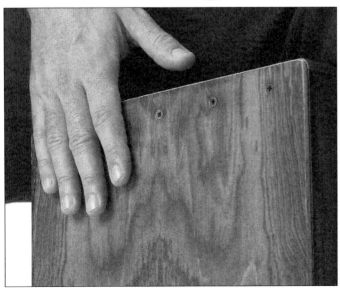

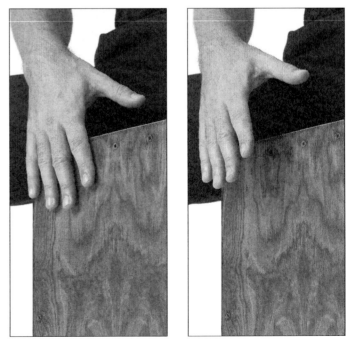

The exercises below will help you develop the slap stroke sound with both hands. Start by practising slowly and focus on achieving balanced strokes with both the left and the right hands. Play the exercises and vary your hands positions slightly until you find the best spot on your cajon for this stroke. Moving the hands slightly higher, lower, left or right can significantly change the sound. The beats are numbered below the exercises to help you keep your position in the bar. You can try counting the beats while playing the exercises; this will help you develop what many drummers refer to as their 'internal clock'.

Snare stroke exercises 1-4

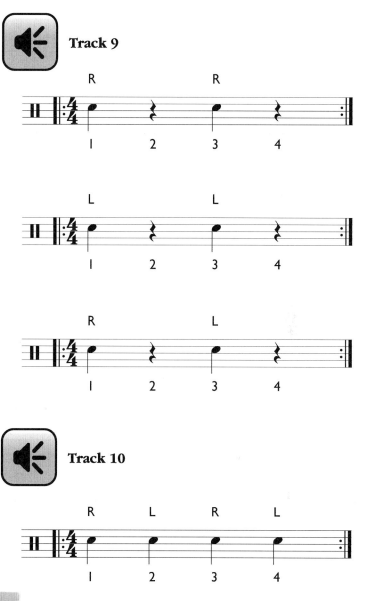

Track 9

Track 10

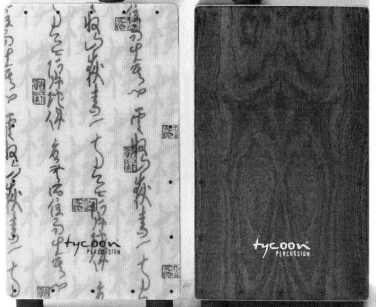

The third stroke: Hi hat stroke

The third and final stroke that you will learn in this book is the hi hat stroke. There are a few ways of achieving the desired hi hat sound and this can vary from cajon to cajon. The basic concept is that hi hat strokes are basically softer snare strokes. This dynamic change can be achieved by keeping the hands closer to the cajon, pulling the hands slightly higher so they are closer to the edge of the cajon or even by applying a gentle curl of the fingers. Experiment and find what best works for you.

Tip
This sound can be produced by the fingers alone too. This will be especially effective if you wanted to play this sound much softer.

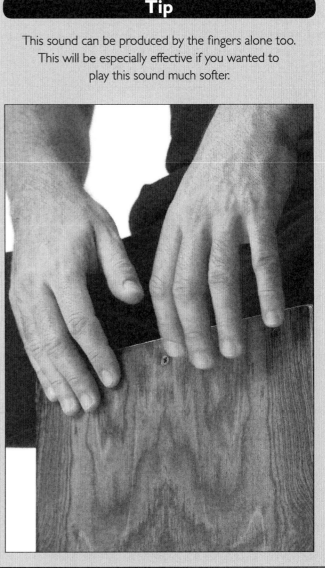

▼ Applying a gentle curl of the fingers

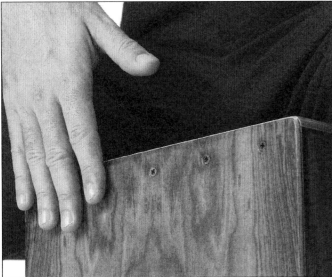

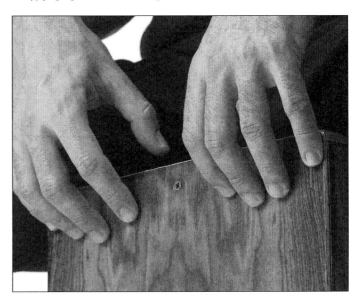

As explained on the previous page, there are a few ways of achieving this stroke. Find what works best for you and aim to produce a balanced sound with both hands. Then, practise the exercises below at various speeds until you feel comfortable with the stroke. Listen to the recorded examples and play along to the provided backing track and your favourite music. This will help you keep a consistent pulse and make practising more fun.

Hi hat stroke exercises 1-4

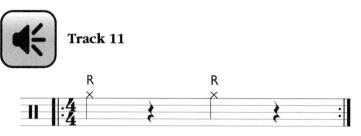

Track 11

Track 12

Grooves: Rock and Pop

On this page you will learn how to put the three strokes together and create your first cajon beats. These beats will be played with 'following' hands. This means that you start drumming with your right hand and alternate hands throughout each pattern. If you are left-handed, start with your left hand. These exercises will use eighth-note rhythms that should be counted **1** + **2** + **3** + **4** + etc.

Basic Rock exercises 1-4
This exercise uses the hi hat stroke, in eighth-notes:

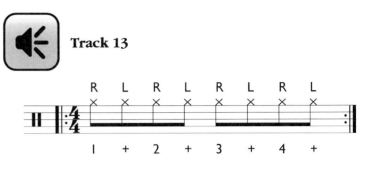

Track 13

Now play a bass stroke on beats '1' and '3' as shown:

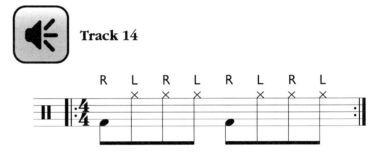

Track 14

This exercise puts a snare stroke on beats '2' and '4' – the 'backbeat':

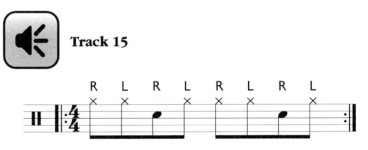

Track 15

Now put it all together: bass on '1' and '3', snare on '2' and '4', hi hat in between to make the complete beat:

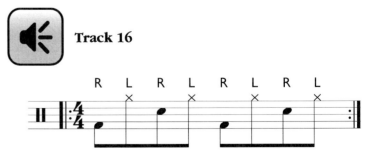

Track 16

Now, let's add some variations to this basic groove. You can play the grooves with a metronome, the backing tracks that are provided with this book or along with your favourite music. The backing tracks are presented in two speeds: at full speed and a slower version. I suggest that you start with the slower version and progress to full speed when you feel ready. The real beauty here is that these basic grooves will fit many styles of music and can be played in various tempos. The backing tracks are to be found towards the end of the music tracks on the enclosed Download Card.

Basic Rock beat exercises 1-6

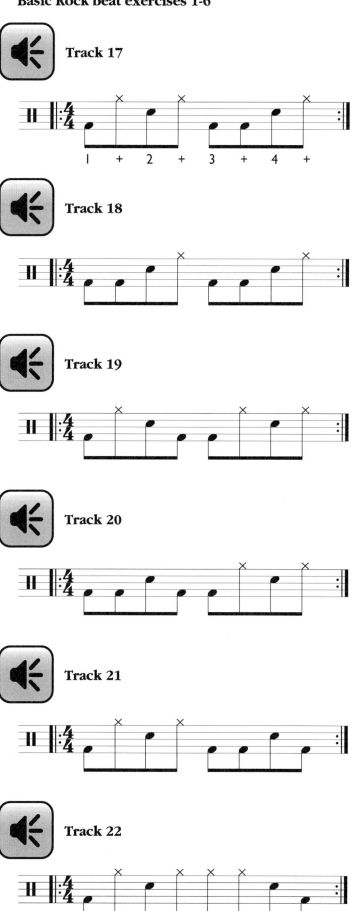

Basic Rock exercises with variations
2 bar grooves

Exercises 1-6

The grooves below are slightly more advanced. You will notice that each groove is double the length: two bars in total. Take the time to work out the variations in each groove before playing along with a metronome.

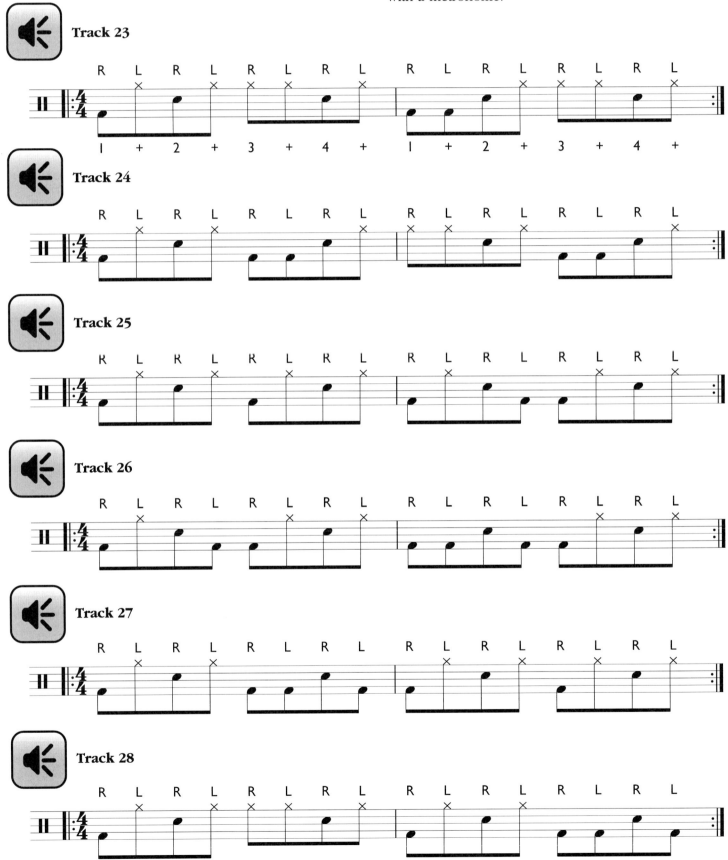

In these examples, you play the groove for three bars and then play a fill in the fourth bar. A fill is a break in the beat, to give colour to the music and usually indicates that a change is coming in the music. You will notice that a repeat sign is used in the second and third bars of each exercise. This means the groove that is notated in the first bar should be repeated and played for a total of three times before the fill is played.

The count below the fill bars will help you understand the rhythms used. The fill breaks the groove and enables you to show creativity. After you master these fills, try to vary them and create your own fills.

Four bar Rock exercises with fills 1-4

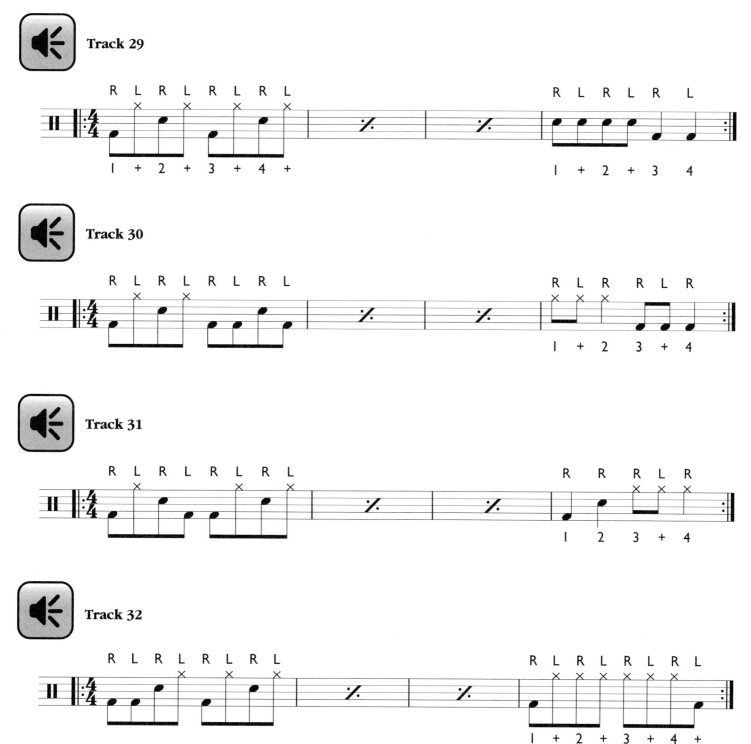

Grooves: Folk and Latin

The cajon grooves that will be introduced in this section are still based on an eighth-note rhythm. However, the grooves are slightly more complex and include some off-beat accents. In an eighth-note rhythm the off-beats are the strokes that play on the '+' of the beats.

The off-beat accents can be played with either the bass drum sound or snare drum sound. It is recommended to use 'following' hand combinations in this section in order to strengthen both arms and develop a balanced technique.

Grooves: Folk and Latin exercises 1-6

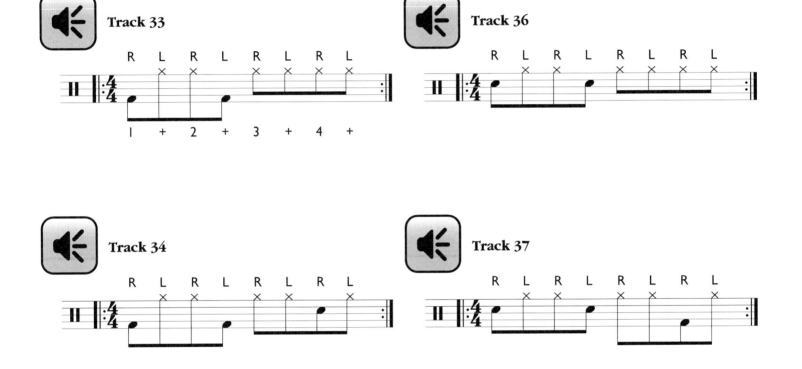

Track 33

Track 36

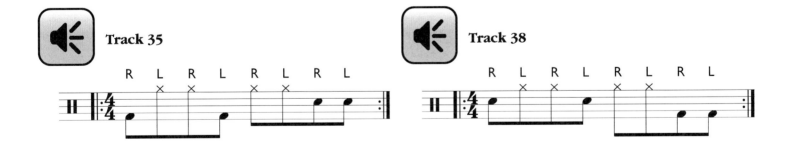

Track 34

Track 37

Track 35

Track 38

Exercises 1-6

Track 39

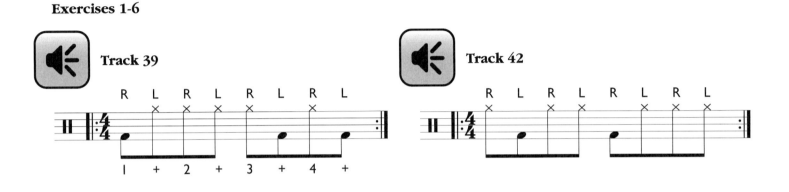

Track 42

Track 40

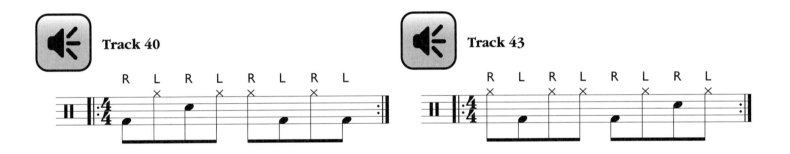

Track 43

Track 41

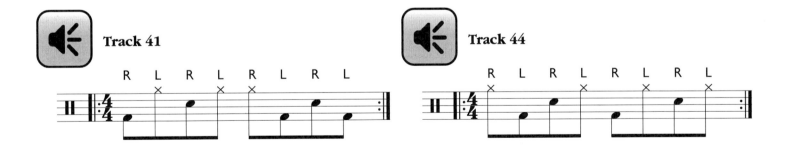

Track 44

Grooves: Folk and Latin

These grooves are combinations and variations of the basic grooves that were introduced on pages 24 and 25. If needed, practise each bar separately first; only when you feel comfortable should you put them together to create the two-bar groove. Choose some folk or world music that is eighth-note based and play the grooves along with the music. Aim to produce a consistent and balanced sound from the cajon while maintaining a reliable posture.

Exercises 1-6

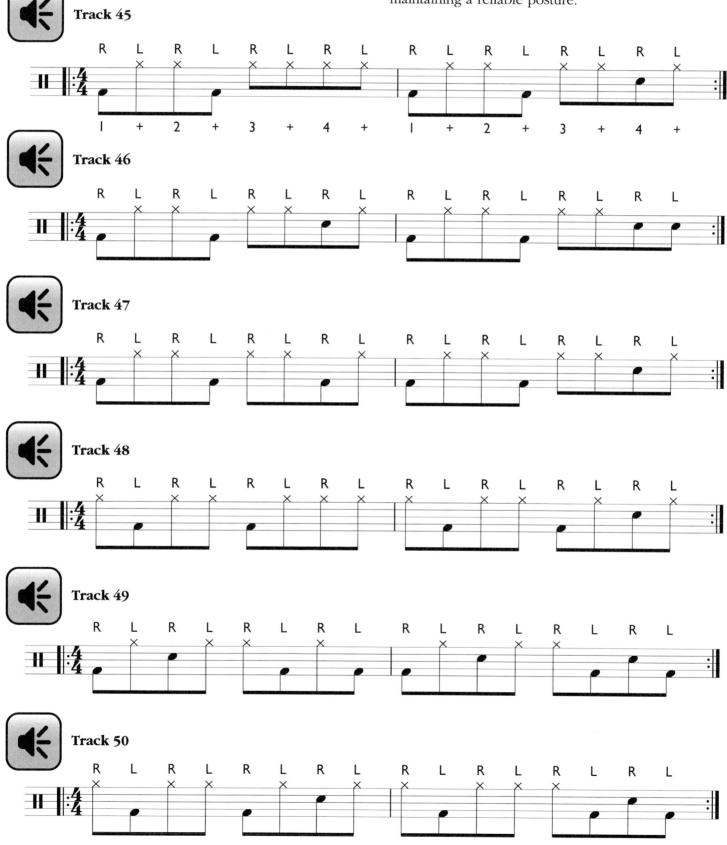

Now, let's add some fills to the beats you've just learnt. Work on the rhythms used in the fills first; the count below each fill will help you. Then, practise the groove and try to memorise it. When you feel confident with the groove, add the fill, ensuring that the pulse remains steady.

The suggested hand combination in the fills can be adjusted according to your technique and personal preference. Play at various speeds using a metronome, along with music or even other musicians.

Four bar exercises with fills 1-4

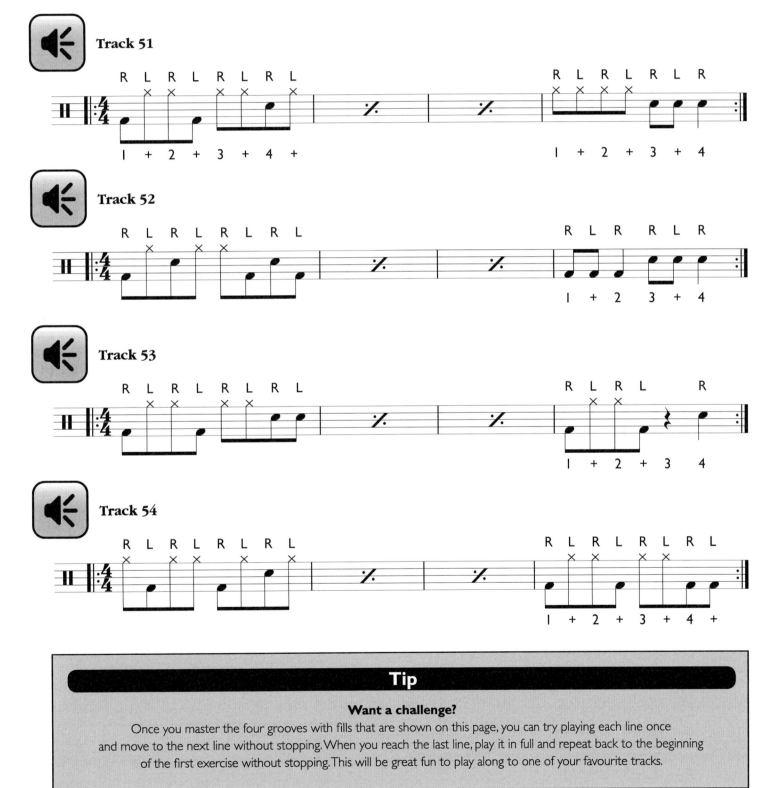

Tip

Want a challenge?

Once you master the four grooves with fills that are shown on this page, you can try playing each line once and move to the next line without stopping. When you reach the last line, play it in full and repeat back to the beginning of the first exercise without stopping. This will be great fun to play along to one of your favourite tracks.

Grooves: Swing and Blues

In this chapter you will learn how to play 'swung' beats on the cajon. Until now, all the beats that you have learnt were in 'straight' eighth-notes which means that all the strokes were even and worth half a beat exactly.

When playing 'swung' eighth-notes the off beats will be played slightly later than before. It's easier to hear and feel this style by listening, rather than from written explanations, so listen to the following examples:

First, swung eighth-notes using the slap sound:

And now the same rhythm but using the bass stroke: Swung eighth-notes using the bass sound:

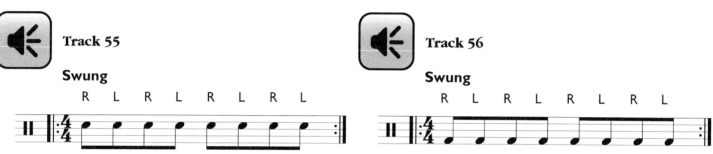

Track 55

Track 56

In the following three exercises, we will combine straight eighths with swung eighths in order to really grasp the difference. Listen to the recorded examples and play along.

Swung eighth-notes, alternating bars using the slap sound:
Track 57

Swung eighth-notes, alternating bars using the bass sound:
Track 58

Combining the two above:
Track 59

Now let's use the rhythm that you learnt on page 28 and play some swung beats on the cajon. The six beats below are as you previously learnt. Therefore, if you understood how to change from straight eighths to swung eighths it should be easy to adjust the beats and achieve the swung feel.

Ex 1-6 swung beats

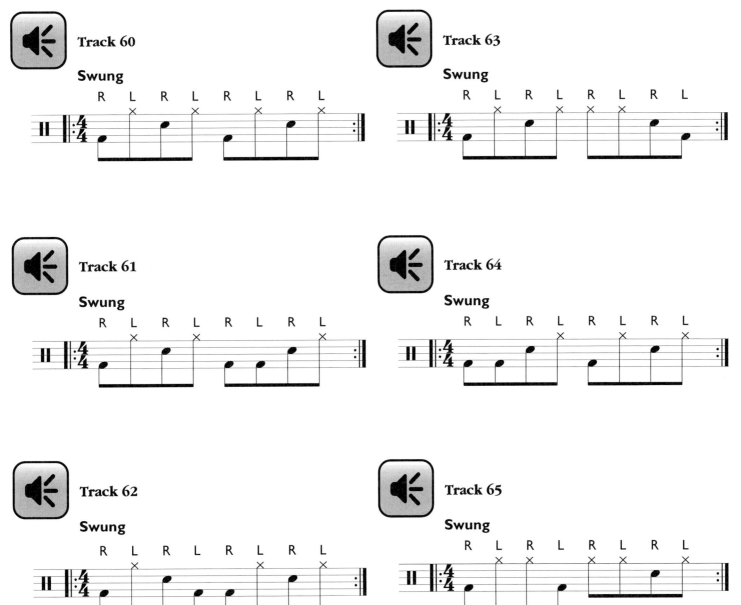

Swung beats

Swung beats can be written in triplets as well. When playing the first and third strokes of each triplet group (and missing the second) we can create a unique, jumpy rhythmic feel. Although the triplet rhythm looks more complex, this is just an alternative way of writing exactly the same beats from the previous page.

Ex 1-6 shuffle beats written as triplets

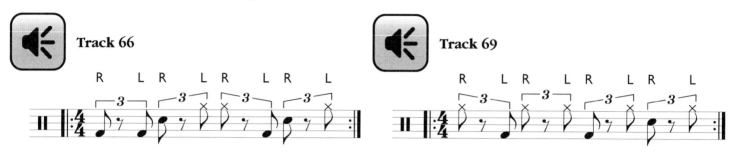

Track 66

Track 69

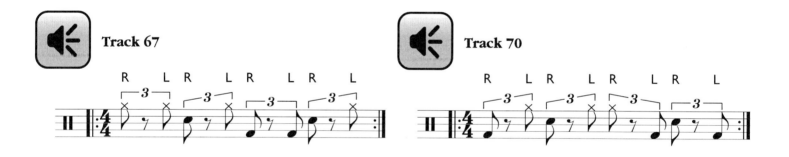

Track 67

Track 70

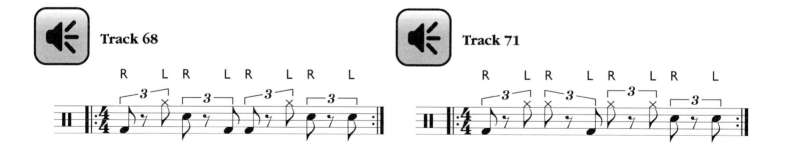

Track 68

Track 71

This 6/8 blues rhythm is slow and hypnotic. We will use a new time signature for this chapter: 6/8 time. In 6/8 there are six eighth-notes in each bar. Practice the exercise below with a metronome (slowly at first) and aim to achieve even and consistent strokes.

We can also play this rhythm using the bass sound.

6/8 using the slap sound

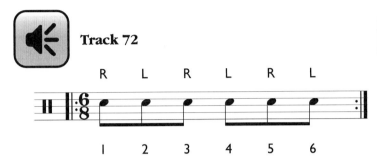

Track 72

6/8 using the bass sound

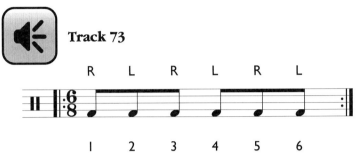

Track 73

Here are some basic 6/8 blues beats. You will notice that the slap sound is played with the left hand in this groove. This is a fantastic opportunity for you to strengthen this hand and ensure that your left-hand slap sound is as reliable as the slap sound with your right hand.

Practise with a metronome or your favourite Blues music until the groove feels steady and comfortable. When you feel confident try and create some of your own variations in the groove.

6/8 Blues beats exercises 1-4

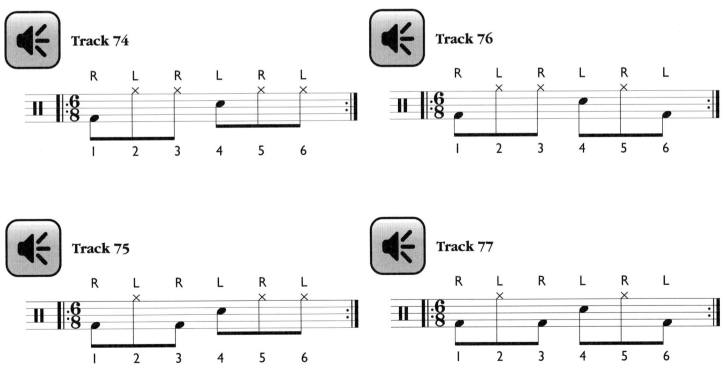

Track 74

Track 76

Track 75

Track 77

Grooves: Funk, Hip Hop and Drum 'n' Bass

Sixteenth-notes

In this chapter you will learn more complex and challenging beats. Many of the beats on the following pages use sixteenth-note rhythms. Sixteenth-notes equal a quarter of a beat and are counted as '**1 e + a 2 e + a.**' I suggest you use alternate hands in these grooves as your right hand (the strong hand) will naturally land on the slap sound when playing the back beats. Here are a few basic exercises that will help you understand sixteenth-note rhythms and the way to count them.

Now, let's take some of the basic rock beats that you already know and play them with the sixteenth-note hi hat rhythm:

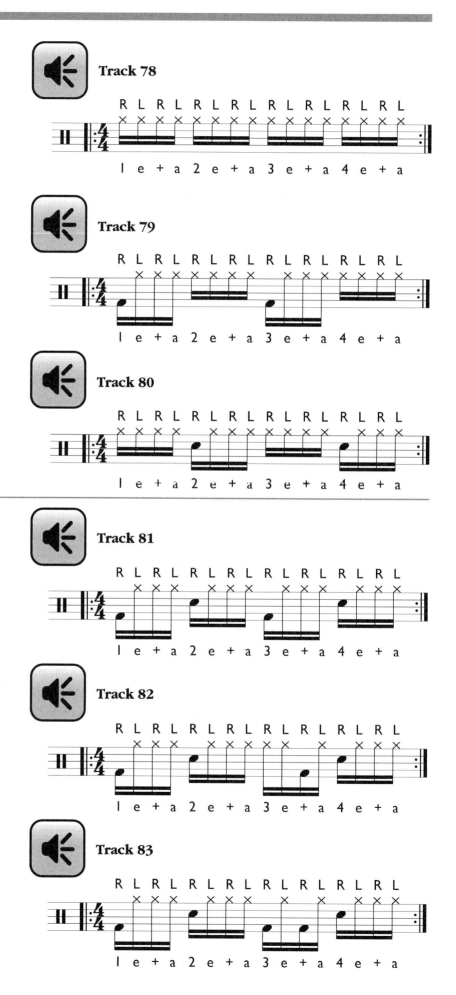

Funk beats are very effective on the cajon. If you master a few of these beats you should always have a cool and funky groove to pull out of the bag if you jam with other musicians. Practise these slowly and pay attention to the suggested hand patterns. Speed up gradually and play with the provided backing track or your favourite funk tunes in order to get the right feel: driving, but relaxed.

Track 84

Track 85

Track 86

Track 87

Track 88

Track 89

Grooves: Hip Hop

The beats on page 33 can also be played with swung sixteenth-notes. Let's try a few exercises with straight and swung sixteenth-notes:

Here are three more cool Hip hop grooves. Focus on the consistency of sound and the swung sixteenth-note rhythm.

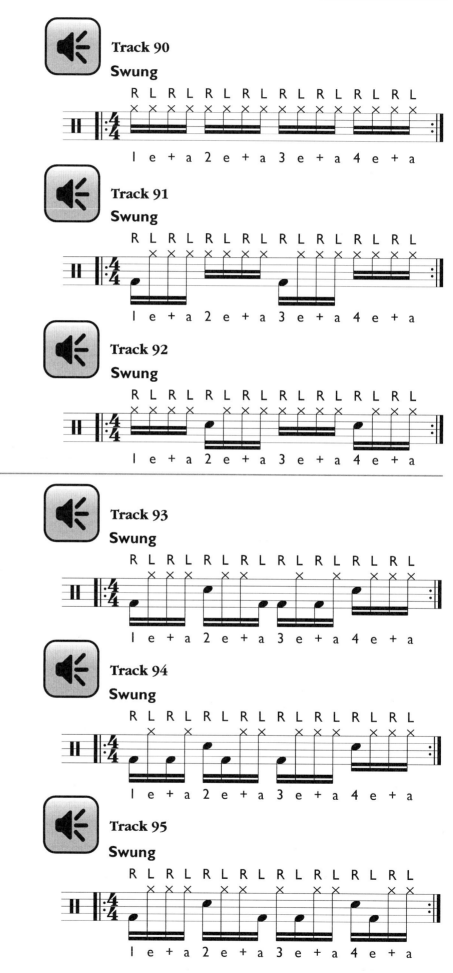

One of the most famous drum 'n' bass grooves is known as the 'Amen Break'. In order to play effective drum 'n' bass beats on the cajon you will need to speed up the grooves that you learnt on page 34. Try to build up the speed of the beats below gradually, and remember that if you maintain balanced posture and remain relaxed your hands will move quicker. The provided backing track will make practise more fun. As always, feel free to play along to your favourite drum 'n' bass tunes and develop some of your own variations on the beats. Although exercises 96-99 are written in straight sixteenths, it is crucial to remember that this genre of drumming will sound and flow best with a slightly swung feel in it. If your technique allows, practise the beats completely straight, then completely swung and then try something in the middle.

You will know when you've got it right, it will just feel like magic!

Track 96

Track 97

Track 98

Track 99

To end this section, we will attempt to play the complete 'Amen Break' on the cajon. This is a four bar pattern with some intricate variations. Practise each bar separately first if needed and put it all together when you feel ready.

Track 100

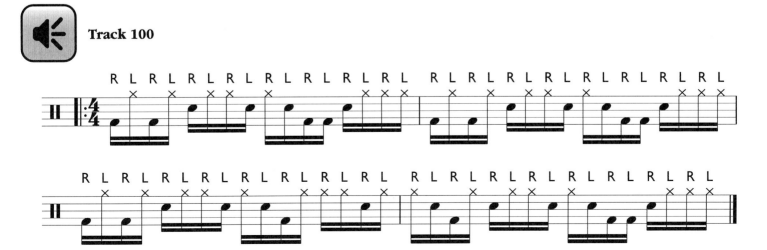

Adding cymbals to your set-up

After playing the cajon for a while you might find that you want to combine it with other percussion instruments to create new textures and colour. Among the most common things to add to a cajon set-up are cymbals.

Splash cymbals

Splash cymbals are the smallest accent cymbals. In a cajon set-up, it can be effectively used to accent a certain beat in the groove or mark a new section in the music. Splash cymbals vary in size, but largely range from 6″ to 13″. Although some cymbal companies produce splash cymbals that are specifically made to use with a cajon set-up, as long as you choose a thin cymbal by a reputable brand it should work just fine. The hand pattern you use will depend upon whether you decide to hit the cymbal with a stick/brush or with your hand. If you hit it with your hand, use either hand as part of the alternating hand combination that has been used throughout this book. If you choose to hit the cymbal with a stick or brush, keep one hand for the cymbal and the other for the cajon strokes. This way of playing the cajon will help you develop your coordination to the next level.

In the exercises below, I will show you how to gradually add the splash accent to the basic rock groove. In the third exercise you will need to hit the splash and bass tone on the cajon at the same time. That will ensure that the energy of the groove is maintained and does not drop. Spend some time finding the hand combination that works best for you. The concept of accenting beats with splash cymbals can be developed to use in many genres.

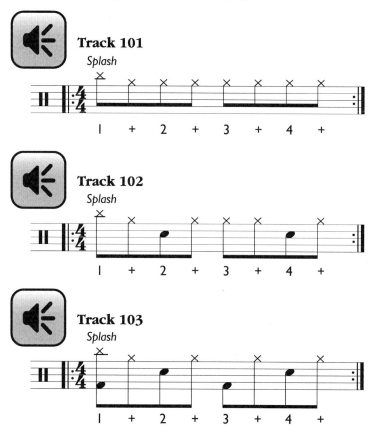

Track 101

Splash

Track 102

Splash

Track 103

Splash

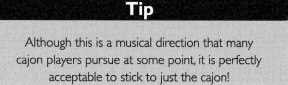

Tip

Although this is a musical direction that many cajon players pursue at some point, it is perfectly acceptable to stick to just the cajon!

The ride cymbal will add another layer of sound to your grooves. It will be used less for accenting, but more for providing a consistent rhythmic pattern in addition to the beat that is played on the cajon. The main challenge is to adjust the cajon groove so it is played with one hand, while the other hand plays the ride cymbal.

A drumstick can be used but might be overpowering, so try using a soft stick or a brush. Both metal and plastic brushes will work and there are many products on the market to try. Brushes can also be highly effective on the cajon itself, so if you get a pair try and play the grooves you already know with the brushes.

Ride cymbal exercises:

Track 104

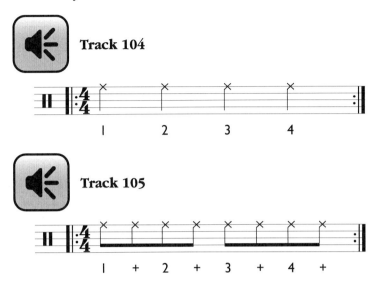

Grooves With A Ride cymbal Pattern:

Track 106

Track 107

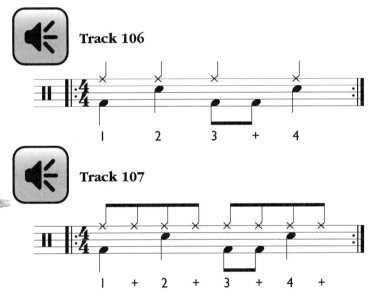

The Hi hat

If you decide to include an actual hi hat in your set-up you will need to look into basic technique for playing this instrument first, especially when using the hi hat foot pedal. In the meantime, the hi hat can be used as the lead percussive pattern like the ride cymbal. You will see that the ride cymbal grooves are also very effective on the hi hat.

The other really useful way of including the hi hat in your cajon grooves, is playing accents with the foot pedal. The accents can be placed on the beat, the backbeat, the off-beats and any rhythmic pattern that you want to emphasise.

Adding percussion to the mix

Shaker

The first percussion instrument we will learn about is the shaker. There are many different types and sizes of shaker but the fundamental concept will always be the same; you need to shake this instrument (rather than strike it) in order to produce the sound. The most common shakers are made out of plastic, wood or aluminium. The size, shape and material that the shaker is made out of will make a huge difference to the overall sound. Most players have a few different shakers to choose from, depending on the style of music they are playing.

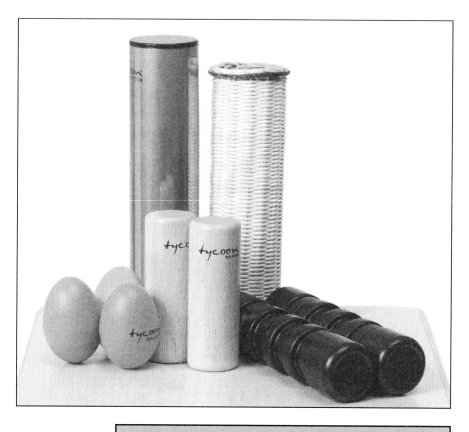

▶ A wide range of different shakers are available.

How to play a shaker

Hold the shaker in your hand, ensuring that your grip is reliable but that your arm, hand and fingers are relaxed and not strained. Start by moving the shaker backwards and forwards; this will produce sound. Now let's focus on the timing of the movement. Choose a speed, set your metronome and practise playing eighth-notes and sixteenth-notes. When you feel comfortable with this technique, move on to the exercises below.

Tip

The tambourine should also be used in a similar way to a shaker. However, the shaking motion of the tambourine should be left and right rather than backwards and forwards. If you are playing Rock, Pop or even electronic music, the tambourine sound is definitely something you want to consider adding to your set-up.

Track 108

Shaker

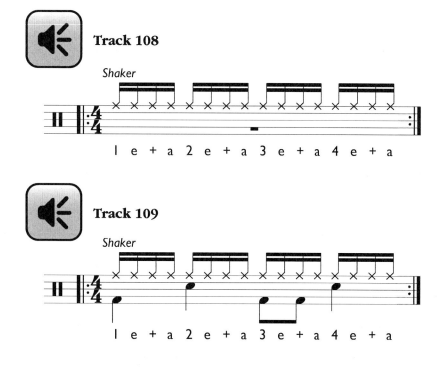

1 e + a 2 e + a 3 e + a 4 e + a

Track 109

Shaker

1 e + a 2 e + a 3 e + a 4 e + a

As the name suggests, this percussion instrument is essentially a small wooden block that produces sound when struck with a stick or a beater. The wood block which is most commonly used in the drumming and percussion world of today is actually made out of plastic. Wood blocks also vary in size and shape so do your research before deciding which one you want to try.

How to play a wood block

The wood block can be played with two main techniques. The first technique involves hitting the wood block with a stick. If you are using a durable plastic wood block any normal drum stick will do. However, wood block patterns will also be effective with wood, plastic or metal brushes. Aim to produce an even, balanced and percussive sound.

In order to use a wood block with your cajon, you will need a stand or a wood block holder. This will allow you to strike the wood block with one hand and play the cajon with the other. You will be able to get these type of holders or stands in any reputable

Exercises with wood block played with hand:

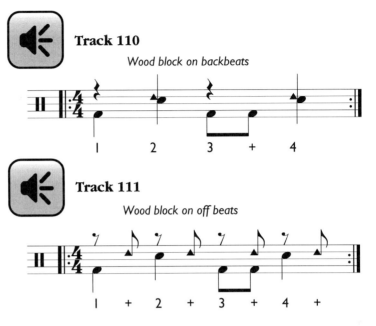

Track 110

Wood block on backbeats

Track 111

Wood block on off beats

drum shop. The wood block can be played with either the right or left hands; try both and choose which works for you best.

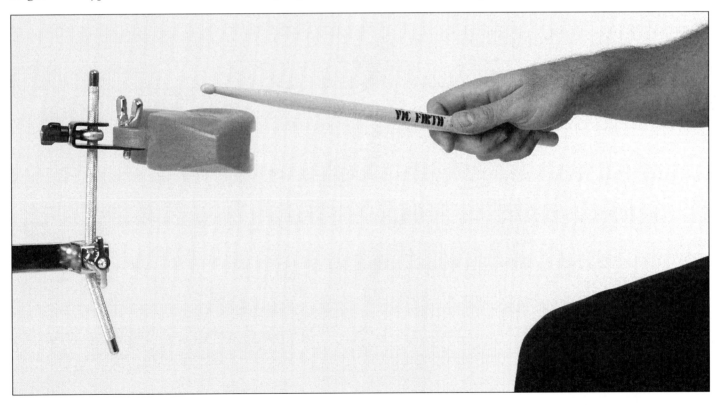

Playing the wood block with your foot

It's also possible to play wood blocks with a foot pedal. It involves a unique bracket and a bass drum pedal (as normally used with a drum kit). This will be a significant upgrade to your sound as you will be able to use two hands on the cajon and make an additional (third!) sound by playing the wood block with your foot. Experiment to see which foot is most comfortable for you to use. Now try to combine the two wood block patterns above with some of the grooves you've already learnt. As your foot will be playing the wood block, both your hands are free and therefore you can play the grooves as you know them without making any adjustments.

Cowbell

Another percussion instrument that can be added to your cajon set-up is the cowbell. The cowbell is very important in Latin music, however it is also common in Pop music, and other styles. The cowbell is made from metal and comes in various sizes; the larger the bell, the lower the pitch it will produce.

How to play a cowbell

Like a woodblock, the cowbell can be struck with a drumstick or played by using a bass drum pedal. Largely, the cowbell projects quite a loud sound. You might want to experiment with softer sticks as well as a normal drumstick as cowbells can be very loud. You will see that the exercises below show how to incorporate the cowbell into the cajon grooves when playing it with the foot. If you want to use the cowbell with the cajon when playing it with the hand, try the wood block exercises that appear on the previous page.

Exercises with Cowbell played with the foot

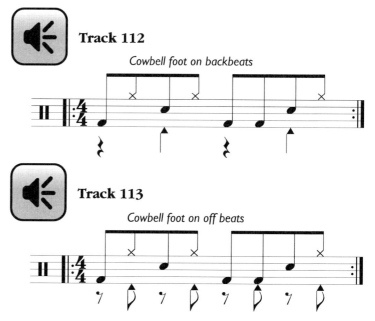

Track 112

Cowbell foot on backbeats

Track 113

Cowbell foot on off beats

This pitch bend foot technique can be challenging to master, but it is very effective and also looks impressive! This can be done with either foot and used in any style of music. Start by playing a simple groove on the cajon. Choose which foot you will use for the pitch bend. Then, place the heel of your foot on the striking surface of the cajon and slowly start moving it up and down. Ensure that the foot always touches the striking surface with enough pressure to create the pitch bend effect. Now, you should already hear that when the foot goes up the pitch bends up, and when the foot goes down the pitch bends down. If you are playing the cajon and moving your foot without hearing any change, try adjusting the location of your foot and pressure on the striking surface until you start hearing a pitch difference.

 Track 114

The musical use of this technique is limitless. Focus on achieving the pitch bend without compromising your posture or a consistent pulse. Then, try to play the grooves that you learnt in this book adding the pitch bend technique when you feel it is appropriate. When you start using the technique ensure that it is used musically, without overdoing it.

Performance piece 1 (cajon only)

In these performance pieces you have the opportunity to mix the cajon beats and styles you learnt in this book. The first piece is purely a cajon piece with no added percussion, so you can really focus on the sound and feel of each groove. The piece is clearly divided into sections; this will enable you to break it down and work on each four-bar section before putting it all together.

In order to ensure that all the styles sound convincing there are a few tempo changes. The tempo changes are clearly indicated in the notation as well as programmed into the backing track so you do not have to worry about it: just follow the track. When you can play this piece with the backing track, try adding your own variations and develop your personal cajon sound and style. Good luck!

 Full Demo: **Track 115**

 Backing Track Only: **Track 116**

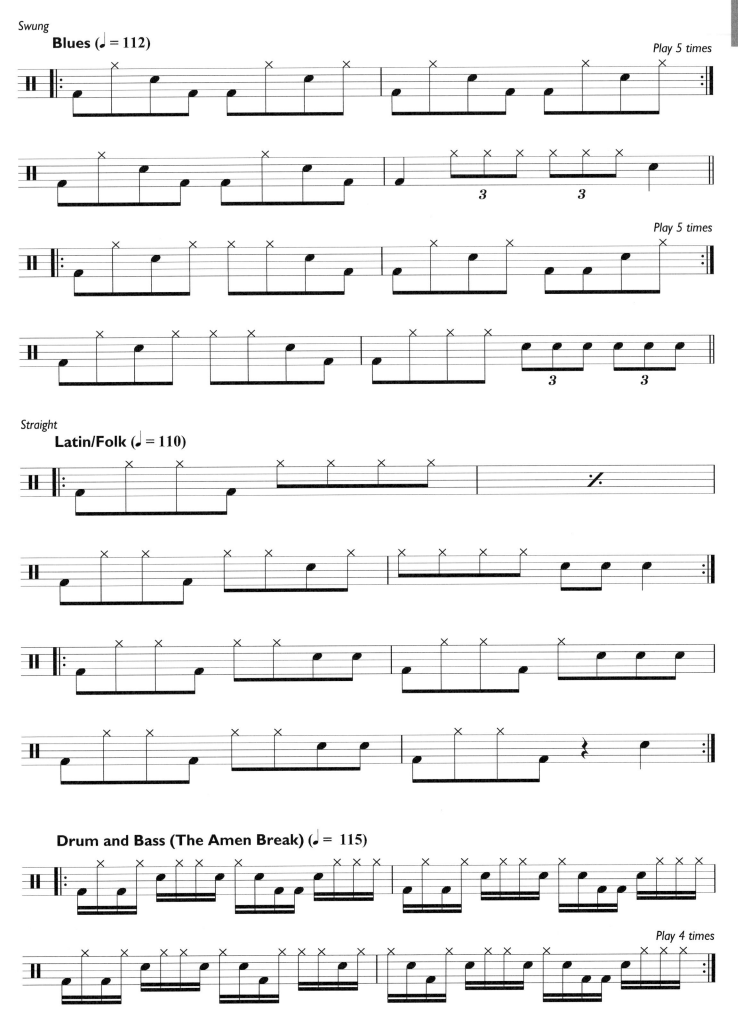

Performance piece 2 (cajon and percussion)

In this second piece you will combine some of the cajon grooves you have learnt with added percussion. In order to perform this piece as written you will need a shaker, ride cymbal, splash cymbal, tambourine (played with hand) and wood block (played with your foot). However, feel free to vary the notated percussion according to your set-up.

The backing track of performance piece 1 is the same for performance piece 2 so when you have mastered both you can switch between them as you wish. As always start slow and build up speed without compromising the sound or the consistency of the pulse.

Full Demo: **Track 117**

Backing Track Only: **Track 116**

Rock (♩ = 97)

Ride cymbal with brush or stick

(2°) prepare for the next section

Straight
Funk (♩ = 97)

Shaker

(2°) prepare for the next section

Miking your cajon

It's best to get the right sound out of your instrument first. Place it by a wall or corner, and preferably on a reflective hard floor to get a good sound. If you're in the studio solo, use a single, distant mic (full-range capacitor is best) to capture its natural sound.

For the front surface, a cardioid capacitor mic works well, with the best position being just below the top edge of the box, pointing downwards so that it aims at the centre of the playing surface. It's a good idea to experiment with placement of mics and different recording levels to see what works best for you.

Recommended Artists

Alex Acuna
Ross McCallum
Rubem Dantas
Caitro Soto
Mario Cortes
Nina Rodriguez
Stephan Maass
Felix Campos
Angel Morales

Alex Acuna

Nina Rodriguez

Ross McCallum

Caitro Soto

Noam Lederman is a highly skilled drummer, composer and author. Having graduated from the London Guildhall School of Music and Drama, he has built up a very successful music career combining performing, composing and writing.

While playing with the Guildhall School of Music and Drama big band, Noam worked with renowned musicians such as Billy Cobham, Dave Liebman and Kenny Wheeler. He then went on to work with top artists and producers such as: Corinne Bailey Rae, State of Bengal, Mark Hill, Trevor Horn and many others.

Noam has taken part in prominent UK and international music festivals such as Womad, Glastonbury, Reading and Sonar as well as appearing on MTV. Throughout his career, Noam has recorded many studio albums, toured around the globe, and been involved with writing and developing over 100 books and various music education methods.

Noam is an academic consultant and drum specialist, and as previous Chief Examiner for international music board Rockschool, he developed and produced their highly successful 2012 syllabus. Other works include the *Hot Rock* series for drums (Rockschool), GCSE performance drums (Rhinegold Education) and more. Noam's collaboration with Music Sales has been consistent and fruitful over the years, including play along books featuring the music of: Led Zeppelin, AC/DC as well as the top apps *Killer Beats* and *Freestyle*.

For more information or if you wish to contact the author please visit his website:
www.noamlederman.com